THE NOISE OF SILENCE

ROHIT KUMAR DASH

Made with ❤ on the Notion Press Platform
www.notionpress.com

Lt. Sushila Dash

Dedicated to the sweet memory of my loving mother Lt.Sushila Dash who too was a source of inspiration for my poetry.Infact I inherited poetry from her although she never wrote a single poem during her lifetime.But she knew all the measure poems of our time.She was an ardent lover of Bhajans(religious songs).She read all great scriptures like Ramayana,Mahabharata,Bhagbat Gita and so many others.She was chanting mantras and singing beautitiful Bhajans till her last breathe.

MAA! today you are not with me.But I am sure you will be showering your blessings on me from heaven till I am here on this earth.Feel so helpless without you MAA!Love you!

Your's Loving Kid
Rohit Dash

Contents

Contents

Foreword

I have nothing more to say. Whatever I wanted to say are already said in my poems. If you read and get what I wanted to convey, it will be enough. Why shall I waste your time by speaking extra. Who in this world has unlimited time today. wish you all a pleasant reading.

Rohit Dash

Acknowledgements

I am thankful to the editors who have been kind enough to publish my poems in their esteem magazines and national and international anthologies.I am thankful to my readers who have been so nice to me and have always remained a source of inspiration in my creative jouney. Many facebook friends have commented so inspiringly on my works while I have postedmy poems on my face book wall .That has encourgaed me always to write more .With ample love and affection I acknowledge the guidence and technical support of my two sons Prasim and Pritish for publication of this book.With out them it would not have been a success.I thank team Notion Press for their timely guidence and support.Thank you all to be a part of my creative journey.

1. The Theory Of Life

Where does life ends?

Does it really come to an end.

I am not a philosopher
Nor a guide
Neither your friend
To tell you wrong or right.

May be life ends
And still there is a
Life after life
It is not me
What they say
That is written
In their scripture
That too is a heresy.

I lived life my way
And never bothered
About what they say
You cannot live
Nor can enjoy

If you listen to other
Hence never bother.

Life is short
The road map is clear
From birth to death
It is thy worth
It is thus a journey
Matters how you travelled
What you did for other
What other did for you
What they said about you
What is said by other.

I can't help
If you still can't get me
I would not suggest
You to read books
Nor would direct
You to believe in any theory
Life is what you live about
And not what is written
On some one's dairy
Hence just go on living
Without much thought
And do not atall worry.

2. The Evil

The more I speak
More exhortion
My speech need
No elaboration.

Still you make
Me to speak
Speak about
The whole civilization.

Whenever I have
Tried to speak something
I have become dumbfounded
Also I feel I have been wounded
Yes that was too the case
With the father of the nation
He thought for the country
But no one could get his emotion
This is the greatness of our civilization.

Yet some people think
Mahatma was wrong
He was shot dead

While he was about to
Sing a prayer song
Three bullet
In his chest entered
Hey Ram! was the last word
He uttered.

What about those
Three monkeys
He patronized ?

Are they still there
Beseeching those truth
One closing eyes
The other mouth
And the last one
Closing his ears.

Do not see ill
Do not speak ill
Do not even hear ill
Someone someday may kill
Telling those evil.

3. Confusion

I have a lot of
Confusion these days
And this confusion
Made me a poet.

Like I am yet to know
About God
His presence is still a big
Confusion for me.

I do not know
Many things
Like I do not know
From where came the earth
I do not know where
From came the sky
The rivers ,water,mountains
Animals,birds
I do not know the chic first
Or the egg
The seed first
Or the tree
To think about it

You are still not free.

This ignorance
Made me to think
And this thought
Led me to confusion
And meantime
In search of my answers
I spelt words
Which people named
Poems
I am not sure about them
I am still in the same
Confusing game.

I do not know many things
I am yet to understand love
I am yet to know
How to love or seek peace
It is not my dish
Still I swim in a troubled sea
Like a fish
And confused about my wish
In the vast world of knowledge
I am only a little dwarfish.

And when with confusion

I utter some words
People say them poems
And me a bard
But my real voice is
Yet unheard
And if in fear of being
Over rated I
Keep mum and even
Do not utter
People still appreciate
My silence
And call me a philosopher.

4. Who Is Not A poet Here

Who is not a poet here.
What
If I could not write a poem
Nothing to worry
Not that everyone
Will write a poem
Not that everyone
Becomes a poet.

See! at the top
Branch of the tree
A bird is singing
See from that top
Of the mountain
A river is flowing
See in that garden
A rose is blooming
The rain too is
Showering with a
Musical note
The cuckoo's coo

The cats mew
All are poems
You should have a
Heart to understand
You should have an
Ear to listen to them.

Who is not a poet here
The nature herself
Is a powerful poem
Who sings songs with
Beautiful rhythm
You should only have
Faith on them
They are at times
Lovelier anthem
You do not need a
Pen always
To write them.

5. The Prayer

I have no issues
With you dear God
Nor any problem
Just for that do not think
I ignore you or blame.

And not praying you
Do not make me
Any difference
Thus you were never my
First preference.

Yes! I was standing
In a queue
In the temple premises
Although with folded hand
But not with any wishes
Not uttering any prayer
Nor in hands with coconut
Or flowers
Not lit any incense stick
No red vermilion for
Your head

No sandal powder
Nor any flower
Standing just
Without any desire.

Even if I visit
To your premises
And am asked to
Pray with folded hands
I forget all the prayers
Truly my heart does not
Have any desire
I forget to beg you for
Anything material
For me a prayer is
Immaterial.

6. Full and Final

Nothing is full and final
Nor what I find
Nor my findings
Nothing is so binding.

You are not supposed
To admit what I say
Nor me what you tell
The world is still a mystery
Without a head or tell.

Mere illusion
What they say
Illusion
Even due to
Lack of vision
Have a revision
Of what you see
Tell and gossip
World is now only a
Drowning ship.

Still let me have faith

On what I see

Let me have faith

On what I perceive

If I am saying

Anything wrong

Please ignore it once

And given a chance

I will never sing a song.

7. The Song Of Solitude

I was all alone.
I was in search of peace
Tranquility.

The world is so disturbed
It is difficult to find
Silence now a days
The roads are busy
The street noisy
Even the sea is roaring
The birds have forgotten
Their songs
I sang a song for myself
Which too was irritating.

Where is peace
Where is everlasting peace
Where is tranquility
Where is that lap of nature
Where I will take shelter.

For our benefit
We cut our jungles

We sold our mountains
To contractors
To make pitch roads
And buildings
They fixed there dynamite
Which disturbed our peace
of mind.

Now we are in search of
a place of that kind
Where is that song
That we heard in silence
The music piper
Bustling in the bamboo trees
Where is the song of
Those lost birds
Who lost their life
In mobile towers
Now the river is dry
The sea is rowdy
The sky is cloudy
The air dusty
The world is so rusty.

Man is sitting all alone
In a lonely beach
Singing song of solitude

To solace himself
The sky too has
No rain to weep
To show sympathy.

The earth has grown old
Man is all alone
Man used nature
For his comfort
Thought himself the
Owner and winner
Now in pain
Thinking of loss or gain
Can't repair the loss again
All cries now in vain
Sings a song of solitude
In pain.

8. Desire

If you have desire
You suffer
But can somebody
Live without any desire.
This is human nature.

If you have a desire
You will surely want
To fulfill
If you fail to fulfill
You will feel ill
You can't bear
Hence you will
Surely suffer
This is what I want to say
But you may differ.

This is what Buddha
Too preached
But I am a common man
I did not take penance

Nor deeply meditated
Please do not believe me
If you not see anything useful
In what I stated

I only stated what I lived
And felt
I told it of my
Experience
But if you take it
Seriously
This can make a surely a
Difference.

If not always
At least try for once
May it work suddenly
Also by chance
As there is no harm in
Applying
They only win
Who go on trying.
Try to live without desire
Living without them
May save you from
pain and suffering.

9. A Word Of Love

The world has
Already suffered much
Due to lack of love
No one is now using
A word of love
Hatred everywhere
We do not now have
Faith on each other
Even some are turned
Enemy
Who were our
Friends or brother.

No peace anywhere at all
Discontentment everywhere
The minds are elsewhere.

We fought with each other
for money
Fought to acquire wealth
And in the whole struggle

Lost our faith.

Even what was required
Was only a word of love
We needed only little time
For other
But we were so greedy
But the world is now lost
Due to lack of love
And now you can not
Restore peace
Even if you bother.

10. Silence Please

I am so tired
So exhausted
With everything
Please leave me alone
I need a break.

Let me live in silence
Let me not utter a
Single word
Let me first shutdown my eyes
Then my mouth
And my ear
Do you hear?

The birds are
Still chirping
It is very irritating
The street dogs bark
In a loud note
The crow cry in
a harsh tone
Even the tick tick sound
Of a lizard of the room wall

Is intolerable.

The sound of dropping
Of a pin on the floor
Is unbearable.
Please let me live
In peace
I need silence
Do not take test of my
Tolerance.

11. I Am Not Inside Me

• 23 •

I am always inside
Myself
I always stay
Inside me
And come out of
Myself
Very rarely.

Sorry if you can't not
find me
I am not exactly
What you see or feel
Or perceive me to be.

You are yet to see
Yet to feel
What am I
I am not exactly
What you see.

Nor what I
Seem to be
Nor the fair skin

The dazzling eyes
The dirty body
Weak limbs
The black hairs
The body worn
With beautiful dresses
Is not me.

How can you find me
When I am yet to
Find myself.

From my childhood
I am in search of a
Man who stays
Inside me
And commands like a king
Yeh! I am yet not sure
About his identity
And has lost my
Whole life
In his search.

Even at times I feel
I am not inside myself
I doubt about soul
Doubt about this self.

12. The Unheard Song

Who were they
I was in search of
For whom I sang
Thousand songs
Spent whole life
For them
But could not know
What was wrong.

They can never hear me
Nor they can ever find
As I am always
One of my kind.

My songs were
Meaningless
As I sang for
Them for whom
It was worthless
They were all
Wrong persons
For me it was an
Aberration

They neither had
An ear to listen
Nor a heart to bear
Then how could
I expect them
To hear
Hence to sing was
Meaningless
And telling them to
Listen was useless.

Then I wanted to
Take a break
And diverted myself
And concentrated
On my inner self
There sat my soul
Cool and silent
On my interference
He became vibrant.

13. Sufferings

I am destined
To suffer
Your opinion on me
May differ.

Most of the night
I do not sleep
The wound in my heart
Is very deep.

I know I will never
Get peace
Even if I wish
Nor any God can
Help me
Thus I too have
Lost my trust
There is nothing for me
So august.

Not that I have
Not tried to come out
Of my situation

Despite all my efforts
I am unable to reach
My destination
That is the sole cause
Of my frustration
Do not know
What can bring
An end to my endless sufferings.

14. She Too Was A Woman

She too was a woman
Who was none other
But my mother.

Who has now become
A twinkling star
In the sky so far.

Who made me sleep
With her sweet lullaby
And taught me
"Twinkle twinkle little star.
How I wonder what you are".

Now really I wonder for her
No more I could hear her sweet lullaby
My voice too does not reach to her
She has gone so far
Which song can bring back her.
(This poem is dedicated to my Mother whom I have
lost recently)

15. Women! I Owe You So Much

I owe so much to you women.
You brought me to
This wonderful world
For you only I could see
Daylight
As a sister,mother,daughter
Friend,fience,beloved and wife
You have always remained so sweet.
You too are tactful
In all your behavior
You are borne to be
A savior.
For this whole humanity
As a woman
You have always a separate entity.
You are far superior to a man
I owe you so much women.

16. Untill How Long

There is no solution
For this endless pollution.

We are grasping for
A breath of pure air
The leaves of the trees are
Covered with dust
Even trees are rare
There is forest
But not at their best
We sacrificed them
for industrialization
In the name of civilization.

The rivers have dried
the clouds have no rain
Birds and animals are
In real pain
For their benefit
Everything is misused by men.

The birds die
For the mobile tower

The sun does not have
The strength
To make bloom a flower
For the vibration
For the radiation
We lost in nature
Our most beautiful creature.

The monkey do not get food
And frequently seen
At our courtyard
For their livelihood

Tiger became a rare specie
People are in search of them
To write a thesis
They are no more found
Even in zoos
Still we proudly use
The mask of tiger
And use their images
In our dress and shoes.
There is no rain
land has become barren
For excessive use of pesticides
There are no insects
Due to insecticide.

The air is not pure
Purity of water
We are not sure
No reason to blame the nature
The earth is no safer
For any creature.

Still we hold seminar
In the name of protecting
Environment
When we have already made
A waste of it for our enjoyment.
But still in the name of
Environment
In big hotels in Ac rooms
In the name of seminar
We still sing beautiful song
But we are still cheating ourselves
And we do not know until how long.

17. Possession

What do you possess
That you do not have to leave
During the final procession
But now as you could not possess
You have so many obsessions.

It is not new and is already
In the saying
That you came naked
While going
Not even the piece of cloth
You are allowed to take
What to think of property
You earn or is your stake.

Still oh men
You feel proud
You are jealous
You are arrogant
And shout so loud
You feel yourself
Greater than other

You are at height
Still for small silly things
You daily fight.

What happenedin Mahabharata
Our great Epic
For arrogance of a prince
And blindness of a king
A great war was fought
And in the war the whole dynasty
Were killed.
In a battle between
Good and evil
The good won good will.

What then we learned
From our past.

Let us then not run
After possession
Let not possession be
Our only mission.
Let us possess those values
Which will be useful
Till our last destination.

18. Yet To Write

I am yet to write
Or what I should write
Whatever I want to write
Whatever has been written
Till today are only my
Emotional outburst
To my feelings only
I have given thrust.

I have yet to write
So many things
Which I daily feel
My feelings and my experience
But I am only busy
Till today in my
Emotional exuberance.

You can always write
What you wanted to write
Everyone in his life
Is experiencing
The same fight

Do not take it light
We must represent
The human plight.

At times it is our pain
At times it is our pleasure
For which a man feels
He lacks in leisure.

Do you really live the
Life you want
Life is only a God's grant.

it too is very hectic and short
So let us not waste it
With useless thought.

19. My Valentine Day

No it was not valentine
While I made her mine
But still we made love
And till today we are fine.

We loved and got married
Despite protest of the whole earth
As she felt I and I felt her
Each other's worth.

Who cares for the world?
Once you are in love
In love you only have to care
For your sweet darling dove.

Now we celebrate love
With our grandchildren everyday
For us now everyday on earth
Is a valentine day.

20. Not Every Time Is Poetry Time

Not every time is poetry time
Nor you can any time chant a hymn
Sing a song or recite a rhyme.

Poetry has its own time
She will get down and kiss
You with her tender lips
While you are unprepared
It will come to you
As a surprise
And may ask you for a byte.

You do not have to
Wait for it
Nor you have to invite
It will not come
When you want to recite
It may come in an
Unknown moment
While you are unmindful
You do not have to judge a poem
Whether it is useless or useful.

It may come in busy moment
While you bathing under a shower
It may come to you while watching flower
It may come and disturb you
While you are on a bike
And show her power
At times poetry may soothe your soul
While your heart is burning in fire.

Please do not play with poetry
Nor deal casually with her
Poetry is not a children's game
Hence handle it with care.

Let me now end my rhyme
Not all time is poetry time.

21. Competition

I am not in competition
With anyone
Nor any one should be
With me
Competition is good till
It is not unhealthy
And they make a foe of thee.

I go on doing my work
That may bring me fame
By doing so many good works
I may earn name and fame.

But without doing any good work
How do you expect such things
Follow my foot print either
If you want to be like me.

Mere jealousy will not take you
To anywhere
In the name of all God
Today I swear!

The world is busy today
In a cut throat competition
And if they fail to achieve
Like others
It brings in them frustration.

That is why in youth today
So many cases of suicide
Whether you will compete
With anyone or not
Now you have to decide.

22. The Deep Sleep

Last night I could
Not sleep
A deep sleep
Although I was badly
in need of it
Heard too someone made
A sound of beep.

The cricket too was
Chirping
The night birds singing
Dogs kept barking
in loud notes
Dispersing darkness
The owl was hooting
The fox were yelping
Wolves were howling.
Frogs croaking
And some mosquitoes
Were whining near
My ears.
I heard a squeaking

Sound of a lizard
Who suddenly jumped
From the wall
I was in real fear
I heard as if hissing
Of a snake from
Somewhere near.

I woke up and found
None to be afraid of
As if they were
All to me
So near and dear
But Alas
I have to fear about them
Those who were cutting my throat
Who pretend to be really
My near and dear
And behave very loving and sincere.

I opened the window
And made a peep
And realized as if
From a long time
I was in a deep sleep.

23. The Worship

I left worshiping
Do not know
Why I felt it to
Be most disgusting.

You too did not
Care about it
Why At all
As you have so many
Who worship you daily
Blindly.

Now I feel relaxed
A lot of time saved
Just calculate
How many time I wasted
On you just for worshipping
You never cared about me
Nor did you do
Whatever I wanted
Rather at times you did
Things as per your choice,

If I asked for something
You gave me something else
If I ask for sweet
You gave all sour
If I ask for a fruit
You offered me a flower.

Thank now I no more
worship
I saved my time thus
And invested them
In poetry
You smiled at my foolishness
And told me atonce
Poetry too is prayer
Worshipping too is a poem
It is like pugating a soul
And dance.

24. My Town

My town is now
no more a town
It is already down
Wearing a black gown
Everywhere man with
Double faces
And the king is wearing
on his head a false crown.

The color of the birds
Are artificial
The song of the cuckoo
Sounds most official
The dog barks at the street
Not on thief
It runs after the pious man
He has stolen as if ?

God is no more safe
The thief has on eye on them
They are stolen and
Sold on a market place
Where God Himself

Cannot protect themselves
Who can tell he is
Secured him.

The night is no more dark
Nor it is fit for a sound sleep
The silence of the night
is disturbed with noises
The morning too is not so
Vibrant
The trees are dried
The sky full of dust and smoke
The atmosphere smells of treachery
There is no smell on roses
How can you stop the
Bad odor of a town
The garbage of a municipality
With few incense sticks
My town now stinks
let us open our eyes fully
And do not only blink.

25. What

What if I do not
Love
What if I do not
Write
What if I do not
Read
What if I do not
Sing
What if I do not
Respire
What if I do not
Perspire
What if I do not
Eat
What if I do not
D What if I do not
See
What if I do not
Hear
What if I do not
Worship
What if I do not

Marry
What if I do not
Obey
What if I do not
Feel
What if I do not
I will be living
Still
What if I do not
Dance
Taaste everything
Life has given you
A chance.

26. Waiting

I am standing
There
Where
Everyday you
Stand
Night
Moon
Star
sky
All the same
But
Time
is different
Your memory
Haunts me
As if
You are
Absent?

27. Arise Awake

All are walking
In their
Walk of life
After they
Wake up
In the hope of
Walking further.

But do not know
Either that
They are
Yet asleep
Yet to rise
Yet to wake up
And has to walk
Furthetr and further.

And are yet
In a fake dream
Deeply drowned
In a sleep so deep
And can't even
wake up

With so many

Noises

So many scream ?

28. Rx.

Take
An
Expert
Advice
Without
any fees.
A poem a day
Keep
All your
Sorrows
Sufferings
Away.
Dosage may
Differ
From person
To person
Hence take
Mediciine
As Advised
By your
Physician
In
Due proportion.

Dr.R.K.Dash.
Make a trial
If you feel it
To be a 'Bakwas.'
(Bakwas is a Hindi word
Meaning useless talk)

29. I Am Greying

With the growth of age
I am greying
But a child in my heart
IS still playing.

To be grey is to be
growing inntiligigent
Means you sre growing
With talent.

It has not been grey
For nothing
Your greying
Says everything

Were you then less
Talented while in black
Now you already cut
So many cake.

But in grey
Your Intilligence

IS some critic's prey?

They take you in light
Hence there future
Stops from becoming bright.

Hence do not ignore grey
For if you lose them
To get you have a lot again to pray
It is what they say
Those who are already grey.

No body grows greuy hair
Oh! no it is not at all fair
If it automatically turns grey
Then only you have the
Maturity in your say?

30. The Globe

World is not a plastic globe
That is used to teach students
In a geography class
World too does not have
Lines on its body like
Ecuader,latitude
And longitude
To mark area
Nor it is made of glass.

World is a place not
Just to live in
And spend your time
World is too not a place
Of criminal to commit a crime
You are born here
Does not give you
Birth right
To hold the world all in your
Arms so tight.

It does not belong to

You only
Nor it belongs to
Anyone solely.

Yes you can make it
More and more lovely
Although it is not that ugly.

World is surely a place to dream
It is also at times so fierce
That makes you scream.

Hence be careful in
All your dealings
It only depends on
All your feelings.

If you want to see
World at its best
Go on working
Hard for it
Without any rest.

Surely one day you will
Get the benefit
If you go on working for it.
So let us not wait for

Things to come
Let us try all to
Make the world awesome.

• 60 •

31. The Enquiry

They enquired
After my birth
From where I came.

Me told
from mothers womb
They asked again
Where shall I go
I answered
to my favorite tomb.

I started my journey
But through out
I was queried
About my name
My destiny
My surname
My caste
My creed
My religion
My belief
I had only one
Answer for them

I am a man
But it was not
Enough for them.

They went on questioning.
I told leave me alone
Let me live my life
My way
Please keep away.
But they never listen
They always wanted
To confine me
With a street
In a house
In a township
In a state
In a country
In a world
But no one believed
While I told
I belong to the cosmos
I am a cosmic man
But they still continued
Giving me pain
They had only
One intention
Their aim was to reign.

32. Taste

Your taste my taste
May differ
I do not know
Even what you prefer
But for that reason
Why someone should suffer.

It is not always
possible to judge
one's preference
In our opinion
There may be a
Minnor difference.
But for that
Disagreement
We will not differ
If we differ that
only we will suffer.

Thus let us come
And be united today
Or else we will be
Missing ourselves someday.

33. Words

• 64 •

I have always advised you
To use the write word
In right manner
Words can give a life
Words sometime
May make a murder,

34. Speak

Speak
Better not to
Speak
But If you have
To speak
Speak always
The truth
Speak a little
Speak slowly
Speak always sweet
It should be
As little as a tweet.

35. Anthem

Try to write

A small poem

Which may

Sound and be

As sacred and sweet

As an Anthem.

36. Pin

If you drop a pin
On the ground
It may not at all
Make a sound.

But if on some one's
Skin you prick the pin
It may bleed
And make him cry in pain.

words too are like that
If your words are soothing
It may be for them interesting
But if you have words disgusting
They may be shouting
Telling it blemishing.

Thus use words
in a discreet way
So that all will be with you
And no one will be from you away.

37. The Bee

One day a
Bee came humming
To my study room
Through the window
And sat on the
Desk top's flower.

I was surprised to see
Her behavior
And asked myself
Could she suck honey
If she could not
I thought!
It is sere waste of money?

38. Immortal

I do not think
Anybody on this
Earth
Has become
Immortal
But There is
every chance
If you are active
On poetry portal.

39. The call

I will not be
Going there
Till I get a call
May be my work
On the earth
Was too negligent
And small.

40. Reading

I do not think
You could read me.
If you think
You have read me
I will not believe
As I know
I have not been able
To write till today
What I wanted to write
And if I tell you
I have not written
Anything till today
You are not ready to
Believe.